Royal Festival Hall
on the    ank

# BLUE FEVER

# *Blue Fever*

### Clare MacDonald Shaw

BLACKWATER
P R E S S

First Published in United Kingdom in 1999 by
**Blackwater Press**
PO Box 5115, Leicester LE2 8ZD

Printed in England by
**Rural Press**
Leicester, LE4 5JT

British Library Cataloguing in Publication Data
  Shaw, Clare MacDonald
  Blue Fever
  I. Title
  821.9'14

ISBN 0 9528557 4 7

# Acknowledgements

Thanks are due to the editors of the following journals and books in which some of these poems first appeared: *London Magazine, Poetry Wales, The Poetry Book Society Anthology,* 1992, *The Observer Arvon Poetry Collection,* 1993, *TLS/Poems on the Underground Prizewinners' Booklet,* 1996, and the *Bridport Prize Anthology,* 1997. Twelve of the poems in this collection were published in *How Ghosts Begin* (Shoestring Press, 1997).

Blackwater Press gratefully acknowledges financial assistance from East Midlands Arts.

EAST
MIDLANDS
ARTS

In memory of my grandparents

# Contents

# Quarry

Hot quarry, the stink of waste.
*Diphtheria down there,* says Nan
to crock-hunters, typhoid smeared

on broken saucers, fish-paste lids.
First prize, a sharp triangle of people,
not everlasting rose, bird, rose.

Second, signed greetings from
potters & sons, old partners in clay
and in ETRURIA, BURSLEM.

Elder's out, fermenting
greensick air. The boy rubs spit
off cupids; she says Nan says

*germs fur up your throat with pus.*
They practise death by glottal stop.
He puts his fractured pink baby

in the shoebox next to its wings,
scraps her pagoda, easy blue junk.
Pollen stifles breath.

Years on, her colds are mortal,
phlegm congeals in septic drains;
sage tea clears it, brewed in Spode.

The dresser's freight – jugs,
sauceboats – is glazedly complete.
She'd let no riveted mandarin,

no half-moon nipped from rim
by time or house-troll
spoil the collection,

but nothing grows in a
china garden. Flung down the tip,
that idle tureen would burst; fission

of painted hearts in nettles, bone shrapnel
piercing sense. Who then might read
fired earth signs, germinal, falling,

inviting to a rococo manganese picnic?
Watteau on Wye; lovers in silver leaf
autumnally flaking.

# Counting

Silence. They've been married
fifty years, known each other
for seventy. Cousins;
nothing left to say.
The window has sixteen panes
of brick and sky
and a dead ash he planted young.
I sit between them
eating raspberry jam,
working out ways to keep them alive.

# Forfeits

The troll under the bridge,
black scratchings in a book,
gives three chances
not to drown.
Goosegirl, white as feathers,
knows its true colour, red,
its name, not to be said
in the schoolyard.
Safe pass this once
over the water;
it will ask again.

New city school; a face
bends down and smiles.
*Paints, books or the band?*
All three is not the answer.
Might as well choose air
sun or sky. No reply.

The hall's clear for battle –
ropes, a headless horse.
*Blues or Greens?*
Too soon to know
the enemy. Back there,
drawing evil queens
held demons off. We
had bloody forfeits,
pins and glitterwax.

*Make some new friends,*
she says. An order. Watch
and pick a greenband
quiet enough for a start.
Tell him he's on your side.
He stares at a robber-girl.
*You foreign?*

Nothing will let itself
be chosen, so why *make up
your mind?* No one tells
you how. Those with the knack
can do quick sums, draw
perfect circles.

Every day
the lightning forks.
Wrong turn, you burn
or end up under the bridge,
your heart torn out.
Yes or no, both go
snaking off the board.
Best not to play at all.

Or learn other ways
of crossing rivers. Drift
down to the ford under
water. Build a spiked raft;
fake your own password.
Trolls are extinct
apart from the one within.
Throw it poison crumbs.

This is what all those
pink-and-whites,
the gold curl winners,
lighthearts at love
and rounders know;

calling *fains* or *pax*
they laugh, escape
a forfeit. No pigswill
down the neck, no warts
chewed off. They won't
get shut in that glass box
to dream a life away.

*Touch wood,* they say,
*cross fingers; it all comes*
*right in the end.* Only
for them it does.

# Sealing Wax

Guano thickens on the lamp,
coral droppings, rock made river
in the sour flame of meths. We hold
stubs to our tin volcano,
building an island.

Her craft is lava. Boils of wax
lanced into veins and leaves
at once turn stone. Umbilical threads
snap from small brooches, mirrors –
our primitive barter, stockpiled

for coasting trade. Back in the war,
house gone, she worked at earrings,
sale or return on emptied shelves; charms
against bombs, necessary vain defiance. Now
she shows me quickhand of wax or paper,

and I make jigsaw rhyme. The kitchen sweats,
condensing spirits from the lamp; forms wait,
sealed in their sticks or coils of tissue.
We open a rose; her scent is burnt treacle,
mine bitter almond, essence of crêpe flowers.

Crusted paste and blisters
deaden the touch. Turning to mineral,
she traps beads on gold hooks with pliers.
Her tiger's eyes have claws. Glass rubies hang
unpicked on the stem: no autumn for stones.

The year of oven-paints I tried out
parrots on ashtrays, wild green birds,
sulphurous, raucous, flat as a page.
I cooked them in pairs; they cracked.
Those days in the quivering tropics

rhyme was easier, rolling beyond
the lagoon. Heatwaves blurred the sight,
yet our mock orchids sold well enough
for the winter passage home. We were
dissemblers, pleasing by artifice,

make-believers. Doubt began in class
where charcoal feet – smudges of bone
and corns – were praised for honesty
above my fervent whirling dervishes.
Fake arabesque; draw what you know.

I know sleight of hand in the dark.
Draining the lamp's purple gin, I
shut art up in its dull room, stopped
twisting guttapercha round wire,
setting words in patterns,

lost power over effigies – molten,
brittle, drawn out of fire – left
for terra firma. She stayed behind,
perfecting unknown species.

# South Circular

The bird on my ashling –
wind-sown  down a crack in the yard –
flies off, won't skirmish with
buzzards, ring-doves, automatic larks
from the humming exchange over the fence.
Their glass cage has burst open with heat.

Wasps are confused;
strawberry air, thick, sweet suffocation,
pours out of jam-factory vents.
Squadrons assemble for reconnaissance,
target me home from school, sunripe,
damp; the laundry steams up our sky.

Buses terminate here,
idle in queues for showers, fume blight
over plants. The last salvia fails
in my mother's petrol-drum, but
commoner marigolds push through sand.
Soil was slabbed over, down with drains.

Becalmed, a sky navy
is hauled in on rigging. Layers of tenants
envy our concrete, quarrel in loud serials
too blurred to follow. From private houses
permitted dogs yap and yap. Water arcs off lawns,
car-menders whistle like thrushes after rain.

We break out.
She finds cool shops. I walk to Southend's
pleasure-boat pond; an island, some thin trees
playing at country. Sky-divers scream, swinging up
and over the turning umbrella; boys in dodgems
bump off canoes. The road roars past above.

Steer aside. Danger
of drowned green hair below scum.
At vanishing point, where cars and water converge,
a broken mill draws me, nailed shut round time.
Traffic stops. Gears unmesh, tar lifts in blisters –
breath of old fields under heavy afternoons.

Birds scold in willow;
don't slide down to before this hot world.
Falling in clouded water, the sun goes out with a hiss.
*Nine,* calls the hook-man, *come back.* His cat
coughs feather and bone. On earth, obedient to light,
traffic starts up. Cool off; take bus to library.

from far places
heard of later in the news. Arms linked.
The hall opened up. Feet should be
travelling on.

# Novice

A body in the bath – it wakes and stares at me
from a quilt. This house is thick with flesh;
armchairs have coupled up in the hallway,
bedding nephews down for the feast.

Jeanne's ironing hangs from prints; old bishops,
foxed by flowering damp raise hands, eyes,
in cloth gardens, deploring their chipped gilt.
She pities my cold land, summers without wine.

Madame's at the station, picking up aunts.
Jeanne drags out glass-crates I'm not to touch.
A chef hired with the silver invades her kitchen.
While she counts spoons, he flaunts *bouchées*

all chicken-scented morning. Upstairs stinks
of smoke-bomb; their factory waste breeds flies
in rusty ponds. Pierre lobs dozens at lunch; his dog
eats the dead, out of courtesy, between thrown bones.

Madame returns. Blackest swathes and hat
set off silk wings uncreasing from the Citroën.
Is it the fiancée? *Mais non!* Why did she run out
last night? Will she be back? I'm sent to the terrace,

where Mlle Lamarche sits by laurel tubs
playing patience with the wind; I fetch hearts
and jacks from gravel. Pierre, behind me, closes in.
No cause for alarm, though – married, at least forty.

He shrugs, joins the massing guests. We sit
on iron lace, looking out. She's spent her life here,
distant cousin, loose thread in the fringe; her brother
died young, *là-bas,* down in their factory.

(Was he . . . caught in a machine? One does not ask.)
A taxi! Voices go speeding up; this is the great return.
Photographers shoo us away, reading omens of light.
Blood-kin burst doors, flow down steps, congeal for albums.

Mlle Lamarche will not face the shutter; she is against
all this. Even so, she would have given the bracelet, but
it was taken, it was lost: *mes topazes* . . . Half-told tales –
asides to a foreign schoolgirl – stick in the brain,

makes them do it? After a fanfare thrill,
the last swallow-dive. We sigh, thin out, trail
off into back-streets, going solo by the canal

where leather Angels mass and wheel, but
can't lift off the ground. Cut through; get
the nerves fit again. Fear's a bad habit.

# The English Jacobin

Cash being short, they let aliens into the *Salon
Vert.* We were their paying leeches, biting
into blue veins to keep accounts unclotted

in the little château, a hunting-box for guns
and horns. If the generator blew, an oddjob man
scythed the grass and sang. I took up jugs

of green well-water bath. Ulrike was good
at bridge, but I trod crumbs into the Aubusson,
handing guests the *petits fours.* While Madame

gave orders below, the older *vicomtesse*
let me read out thrillers, correcting every *r.*
She asked about death duties at home. I said

they were low in our flats. Worked on Bossuet;
his cracked gilt spine let out a whiff of tomb.
When my grant didn't come, voices iced over.

Stuck without cash, I watched for post
like a lover; no work in the village, no escape
from debt. Hid in the shrubbery with Racine

for GCE until the glowworms lit
and flickered out; walked the cabbage fields
on stinking afternoons. Tried to pay some off

in ping-pong or *le chat blessé,* keeping twins
out of the river. At last the Council wrote.
Travel scholars had been sent a grant;

prove its non-existence. By harvest I'd be
grubbing roots. In these feudal times
the boys came home from Bexhill

to show Maman our curious
English habits such as leaving hands
under the dining table. War began

with an unspoken crime. What had I done?
Punctured bikes and scuppered boats.
Something about the English

never joining in. Ulrike declared herself
a neutral zone. Found I wasn't guilty of
but guilty. With every word

I murdered exquisite vowels. Took
vampire walks at night and soured the milk.
Was a spy for the *Syndicat d'Initiative*.

For want of cash, and perhaps for want
of grace, I became their foreign Jacobin,
their bogey. Hated being hated;

they foresaw death and executors,
but I could hear tumbrils coming for me.
A month in the country, studying,

watching lizards run up walls, or rain
at the bedroom window damping
old blue pastorals. Once as they

tuned the radio an English voice
spoke firmly to the world, faded out.
My fault. I chose this exile,

fell in love in the library
with feudal France. Old novels,
guides to the Loire. I'd lived

in a turret at Azay-le-Rideau,
spinning courtly lies, always on
the right side of the moat,

but this was a grey cube,
shuttered; no oriel, arch, or vista
to excite. Still feudal, though.

Madame opened the fête, spoke
down to small girls in lipstick
and shot taffeta folkwear,

wing-headed nuns like flying geese.
My first mass was not romantic.
The *curé* rattled on about

Hitler and the Pope; old politics
in church? Theirs was rather dull –
wrong colours in the glass, no choir

– so I began to listen, learned about
the games of war, and held my tongue.
Madame said my accent had improved

*pas du tout, pas du tout, pas du tout.*
Reading her glances I began to see
my clothes were *incroyables.* Yet

the sons grew kinder every day.
Now she divides the family? Cash came
to free us from each other. Paid, packed,

made a great speech on toleration
to her tightened mouth. Got out my gift,
handmade, brought from home,

but when I saw her hold the earrings
at arm's length, pair of dead mice,
I felt the glass drops turn to blood.

Race, class, *la guerre,* money,
and good taste thown in – a useful
summer school, cheap at the price.

# A Waste of Breath

The drinker shields fine wine from an invasive scent.
Palate numb, he scorns a dissolute thirst for oils
pumped from hot wells in flesh, as pores dispense
legal tincture of opium, atomized proof of spirit migrating,
spice-ghost, *spectre de la rose.*

Slow tongues, learning the grammar of taste,
progress from monosyllables of beer, gin, rum,
to fluency in Châteauneuf-du-Pape. Illiterate nostrils
find no primers for scent's dead language –
nouns like otto, attar, root of calamus, and verbs
for smearing necks over the pulse of blood
as incense swung. Passwords to primitive brain
survive: carnation of flesh, narcissus, old narcotic.
Myrrh's that fungal shadow at the heart,
but whose nose can tell styrax from opopanax,
or censor ambergris, floating vomit of whale?

The alchemist has turned designer, setting out phials
among vanishing creams to subvert. He mixes metaphors
of lily and tuberose, translated to aldehyde, adding
chemical similes of musk. Trapped in stoppered glass,
his compounds flaunt their images; odalisques and amazons
spell out bold civet or milk of vanilla.

Dogs, children, fluent in dung and flowers
need no interpreter. Older senses fade with the green wind,
*Vent Vert,* in a blue hour, preserving dried stems of bouquets:
wine thickened year by year in the hymnbook cupboard,
vinegar air sousing wood and word, or a scarf of chypre
round a mother's neck, faint lilac print on moss.

Scholars teach no art of aromatics;
the good cry rape for lavender plucked and stripped.
Though rosemary oils the brain, and nothing so green as shades
of vetiver will cool the eye, the cynic says, *lilies of the field?*
*– hydroxycitronellal now, a waste of breath.* Do absolutes remain,
quintessences, alcohol for the soul? Exorcise small demons
*per fumum,* burning cypress with sandalwood; keep to the lit path.
Offer the guest a dry cologne, or vintage frangipani
rich as oloroso. Scent the bitters of life? Prepare for disbelievers;
wormwood in vermouth is easier to swallow.

# A Legacy

Dull gods, nameless,
plastered over sky,
snuff the cold breath of infidels
escaped from weekly cottages,
rain, to the great house.

Mortals stare at relics:
cool salami tables
veined with blood and fat,
easy thrones, balding
in the state rooms.
They touch gilt for luck
to flake from cabriole knees.
Beds are tired of marriage;
this old stumpwork tent
has pressed layers of dried hearts
to death by a thousand flowers.

Set free in a wing, the lord
is out of the shrike's glass eye,
divorced from bills and silver.
We're his inheritors;
what shall I do with my share
of time?  Go into the grounds,
my real estate,
this millionth inch of green.

Cliff-hanging gardens grip rock
or slide in weirs of clematis
level by slow level
to basin ponds and underwoods.
Clouds terrace an open valley,
double-arched light running
to wash as fugitive dyes
leach from rain into flowers,
making damp fires of Lucifer,
shocking crocosmia, flare up.

The gardeners drive stakes
into monkshood, windblown,
poison-bottle blue. A cutting,
please, of indigo death.
Get sage, thyme, roots of order.

All paths meet at infinity:
this painted drop for a masque,
shining wet, invites abstractions
to materialize. Virtues descend
through rain to caution me;
stony women lean on urns
enlightening the mind,

until new lovers pass,
fused in a trance; they
are turning elemental,
finding themselves
the first green pair
to flower in a garden.

The rest of us, lapsed
in love, must go. Rich
cities to the east will soon
seduce the disinherited.

# Static

On this ward
everyone's chosen
death in paperback,
murdering time.

Consultant appears,
trailing students. He
pins down malfunction,
tests their reactions

to the live apparatus,
asking for estimates.
Singe nerves? make
cardiac arrest?

Hear his fiat:
cut cable head to
heart; stop current
in blood; next bed.

Moon on lino. Sun.
The nurses came when
I was in my lilywhite hour;
the trolley bore me away.

After gas, body lay
stiff in sheets; saw from
far below, ditch of sighs,
a hand wake it,

fingers to wrist,
metering faint volts. At
visiting time, the cured
black out illusions

who come with grapes
and bunches of words;
many relapse and close
old circuits of pain.

The window tree
catches at quick clouds.
Lie still now, earthed,
remote, in control.

# Undercliff

Ammonites show up
as the cliff splits,

curled snakestones,
clots in an old vein.

Transfiguration:
the chosen, gathered in

from high graves, are
purged by drill and scalpel;

ribs stick out of calcite,
glacier channels in shell.

Risen, buffed to a gloss
and named in a dead tongue,

they shine on a shelf,
crystallized fruit of time.

Backsliders crash down,
shaken from seams –

windfalls to scavenge
and stretch the dole.

Hunters catch brittle stars,
pull the devil's toenails out

at first light, but tourists
want stale fish from Brazil,

90-million-year-old pet
antiques. Agate mats for gin,

a mammoth tooth, or
sharkshit for the guppy bowl.

We all need household gods,
strange familiars. Our clocks

are ammonites; children still
play knucklebones.

At the beach, rattling bogs
of shingle trip and suck

feet into a drunk walk; hot wind
sands you down. Women look out

to sea. Someone's teaching boys
how to acquire, raiding the cliff.

They have knapsacks, goggles,
the right hickory hammer

for smash and grab. Bird-skull
flints go in a bucket; they long

to find some prehistoric bat
stuck in the rock.

Fields above are tilting;
a slow lava of shale

steams and rots below grass.
Coal splits to show twins

curled, self and shadow.
Stone circle, mould, mud,

and over again. Soft forms
like crinoids frond a pool;

the anemone shrinks
as old bones drop in.

No beach resists us,
thieving pebble eggs,

charms to ward off
a cold heart. Clutching

stone, we try to keep
our dead more alive

than this, but they
wear with us to shingle,

loves and selves thinning
to sand blown in the eye.

Fossils give no sign
of resurrection; look

for kinder oracles
than science on a beach.

In the rock-shop chapel
ammonites mass and wait

for our instruction.

# Off Bourbon

Boatman ferries his cat and a heavy master across. They're
hung from a nail to repeat in oily shadow. From the hotel's view
of the past this art goes with iron – chains of balconies, spiked lanterns
over beds, oxblood walls and a pool of blue ink. Tourist now, don't pretend
to be a traveller; live and work in the land a year but alien on the road

in the wrong season. Rain turns to steam in your clothes. An ice-cream seller
won't give rough directions – raped twice down there. This quarter's fine.
Honeymooners eat Creole, buy electric yo-yos, sit for pastel sketches
in the square. Ought to get off Bourbon, see the sights. A straight old lady
looks through glass at a bride – white silk habit on white plush horse.

She catches my reflection, then the accent; get a self back in easy words
with strangers. We count the cost of wedding. Something's dredging up
but drop it for now; cord unreels, a weight falls. Over the tracks to reach
a steamboat hooting it's off upriver. On deck, light is bleach in the eye. Squint
at banks of elevators. Billions in grain, but card-playing sprawls of drinkers

don't look overboard. Back on earth now, what to do? Compare pinks
of myrtle and poison oleander. Find that streetcar. A guide (latch on)
is showing his group the only hill in town – twenty shovelled feet,
green as a grave. But dig a grave and you've sunk a well. Under's over;
a year and a day in a box above ground and your bones are crumbs –

natural cremation – though in this damp heat you'd liquefy. Slip into
a convent. Thrilling chill as it's mouldy, under repair. Some nuns
are curling off the walls; months of heroic exodus from France to this.
Their old charts pock and ripple. The cathedral's in good spirits, turquoise
and purple theatre of saints. Think of Mardi Gras, but racks of fancy dress

on café-show aren't festive – frocks need flesh. Waiter says he wants to
take me round the darker night-sights. Thanks, but I want sounds.
This is an early dive: bare boards, hooks for jackets, and seven old jazzmen
in rolled sleeves and ties. Open-string piano, clarinet, banjo, bass,
trumpet and trombone, down by *St James Infirmary* under a lazy fan.

Hard benches for the devotees, a basket for dollars. A player's lips
and hands stay free though the face has set. Real jazz ends at midnight-thirty,
now for the streets. This quarter's hardly blue; everyone rolls by staring
through open doors past the touts and bouncers and the bar-top strippers;
lust is for icy drink. Here's Mrs E, met over café lunch; her friend

works a nightspot and I'm to come. Laverne in flame stretch
will sing your choice of torchsong. I'm bought three zazaracs on a tray,
can't spell or say them after one. Absinthe, bourbon, rum, though the bar
could be in Birmingham UK. Slow vote of thanks and head for coffee-stalls.
No water-moon where levées box the river in. Feel unromantic, so I'll skip

the slow boat to Mexico, splash out on air. A sky-hop, bouncing off
another soil. Gulf is olive swamp is sea is sandbar; I'm its weather,
high anvil cloud. Silver riverroads shrink as the held storm lets rip,
wipes me out. Unknown, unknowing, drawn into the hum of the plane,
until a steward tries to rescue me. *Bourbon. Or a tequila?*

# American Gothic

Fridges keel over and sail downtown. The store-glass burst at 32 feet,
though Schrader got the sofas muscled upstairs. All year I've sat on his
colonial suites, turned maple or cherry. Kind rooms, open to an alien,

your walls are cracking up. WPBZ alarm: there's gasoline on the flood,
dying for a cigarette. Silence – breath could ignite – till it's drained off.
Small mountains blot themselves back into a wash of sky.

Next day jeep tyres pop, nailed by planks. The unrich flushed out
of timber homes downstream resent us, nosing in with dry papers.
How many people in your house? *Fifteen / No, she's / He's my /*

*Shut your mouth.* Have you an electric fire? *A what? Where would I get
space heaters?* – and the power's off. Dogs nip at mottled ankles,
parked children fight. We dispense milk for babies

in plastic severed breasts, baggy to finger; unstack these horrors
from a greening fridge. Everything's run out, including the pill. Last night,
they say, all the heart-tablets in town blew up – nitroglycerine bombs;

no deaths, but this is how ghosts begin. Did an absent friend's house
survive?. Wade over to see. On every sill a radio pioneers . . . *with Chlorox;
clear gutters, or mosquitoes breed; basements pumped too soon collapse.*

People don't collapse; they deal with rats, gnats, chiggers and ticks, sweep
knots of washed-down copperheads off their stairs, tip up deposit boxes
by the Bank and wring their deeds. The air's ripening dead cats in drains,

but the National Guard is boarding stores; the Navy's sending
a cutter upriver with typhoid serum. It's a very civilized disaster. No one
allows this round to Nature; Bibles fanned on the stoops are warping dry.

Her door was a direct hit – padlock on, hinges off. The river went upstairs
in the low foreign quarter. Before hose and broom, grope the sludge for luck,
but tapes and files have cockled, plates stick up like shells. Put out in the sun,

scrubbed armchairs shrink, twang, bust a coiled gut, and go
on the last free plague-cart after all. Water's been making love to her cellar.
Back at the ranch-house I unlock the trunk, a step-in death-trap,

one of those touring vampire coffins propped in the old hotel.
I planned to float off on it when the dam broke. Boring portables
all safe and dry, but the town's lost its past – yearbooks, letters from the dead.

Clots in the blood of time. Move on! there are no whingers here. The Office
of Emergency Preparedness is gearing up for claims: *The Householder should paint
on a piece of plywood the following: 'Porch Gone: Mr & Mrs John Doe' and place it*

*in the photograph. Size the damage, including a yardstick or broom, or a man.*
All over town hair's being smoothed; the Does are standing like jailbirds with placards,
grave *American Gothic* pairs in front of a clapped-out clapboard house,

waiting for the next life to begin, after the click.

# At Kutztown Fair

you'd buy applehead dolls
dressed in Amish black,
alphabets and proverbs.
The hex-sign maker targets
luck in bright circles

for your barn. Need a
carved eagle or long clock?
Gingham folk will serve you
shoo-fly pie, molasses,
and other sticky treats.

A *land of milk and honey*
says the speaker, but each
tent gives a peepshow
into the hard life of fever,
herbal cures and snake-lore.

There's a crèche for coffins,
ruched satin nests, tall hats
on top for weepers, ribbon
streaming. So blow your egg
and paint it paganly.

Speech inflates itself with
broadcast words as good
as battle hymns: *iron
hand of the oppresssor
from across the water.* I'm

their culprit, tyrant long
removed. Flatten myself
against a stall as the parade
goes by, leading a criminal
to his mock death. We're

hay-high on the wagon
with girls in dimity prints.
On the scaffold, off.
As the billboard says:
*HANGINGS 11am, 4.30.*

Just some waster, after all,
only acting – and we torch
Guy Fawkes. Better not probe
our quaint old sacrificial ways.
Or not right now.

# Looking-Glass

*Chronicle*

In our familiar looking-glass
the histopathologist unwraps Asrū

temple singer, brown-papered bones –
to chronicle her death on the Nile.

His fringed skull bows to hers.
Through the gap of an eye he loosens

a beetle, candied in green resin,
embalmer's amalgam.

Pioneer down cavities, he probes
a silted lung – the sand inhaled

bringing taut vibrato to the hymns
of Amon-Ra. Her faith was half truth:

in the flowering of time she is performed
to the numberless profane.

*Nat. Hist.*

The zoologist, filming Eden,
is shot with catacombed ibis,

wise old birds of Thoth, maturing,
stacked like bottled spirits, to uncork

on nights of doubt, when virtue's slipped
from scarab, fylfot, silver horseshoe.

No mysteries now – clairvoyance after
unspeakable vows in the grove;

arcane knowledge is licensed to all –
costs less than a soul. The glass ignites:

conjured sages explicate
evil as virus, disease as ludo for cells,

but the binding words are lost.
Viewers try *seal again, Sesame.*

*Equinox*

With his phase conjugate mirror,
the physicist, master of light,

reveals a new science of optics.
Three rays converge on crystal,

and one leaps out. He cures
distortion, seems to reverse time.

His art's more threatening to see
than the dance of electrons

resurrecting Asrū; it drains mind
out of its shell, as though

some archivist in future,
scanning the palimpsest of air –

images webbed in fibrous time –
were raising up by hologram

tonight's uneasy watchers
out for documentary truth.

Particles drum down years
in photon tattoo,

projecting for an instant
faint negatives of self,

thin as a slide of Asrū,
film of dust on glass –

a trick done with mirrors
in the brain. Get back

to common time, solid
old reality; shut fear

up in its box again. Power
lies in our hands; take aim:

off with their talking heads.

# Folk Tales

*. . . on the flyleaf?* He thinks he knew
an Elias, not Alice; his own name, hanging
from lower branches, will be squared off
in a year. An uncle's relating folklore
censored by mothers, the source
of pure blood, who'd ban
his greenwood fancies,
cuttings from Hardy.

Cousins, teaching now, and both
hunting the dead, we'd nail his rustics
up our stairs – he's the keeper of
old oak faces, varnished primitives.
*Those women, your grandmothers,*
*what did they make of life?*

The quilt of hearsay left to us
pieced them together, serge and crêpe.
One went sour with righteousness,
teeth into green boys; the other,
said to be kind, held up long bones
at the Bury – ladderback matriarch, donor
of sprung discs to slouching descendants.
And all that puritan humour, flux of zeal,
still leaks from us into margins, footnotes,
purging faults and urging vision.
*Those women . . . ?*

But he can't tell us; to him they were only
corner shadows, thin black house-spiders
hung in old webs. Men could range the land,
sleep in haystacks, learn to engineer,
or roll out of the bell-tower in a gang
after triple bob minor *drunk as owls*
*– never at service, heathens all –*
until new vicars came abolishing
rough cider on the ropes. Bells
no longer stumbled through tangles,
colliding aerially in figures of eight.
Silence rang in women's ears.

**THE POETRY LIBRARY**

Fading out of an Indian sun,
his father blew the last cash on treats
for cronies and a motorbike for jaunts.
Mortgage? Living death; you'd be stuck
with damp, rot and the shame of tick.
*Slaved on his cousin's farm, lugging
great sacks. Housekeeper got it all.*

But I've heard other versions;
no two aunts agree. Were you there
the night he said all this? Did you hear
about the parrot and the ploughing match
when his father, goaded by *you sowdjers . . .
good for nothing,* put on full uniform,
boots, brass, and won? The cash bought
clever Tango from a sailor; it could swear
in oriental tongues. He'd hang its cage
from the apple-tree to keep it wild.
Caught in an icy British draught
the alien died.

No, you say; I told you later.
So another quilt of scraps begins.
Some of them match; we know
there were five young to rear,
four after the croup. Eldest boy,
this uncle, to be day-schooled,
but not his sister, hungry for words.
She put a chair in the wind to read,
pages cuffed by drying shirts,
loitered at the brook to die,
Ophelia, Lady of Shalott,
floating among lilies
down streams of verse.

Her brother turned away from
bloody village life; hardly watched
the rat-catcher castrating lambs.
Grieved by the disorder of things,
he found his father out with the policeman
shooting pheasant – his own catapult, too.
Morally groomed at school, he said to her
*Why are these people allowed to live?*
Yet he begged in vain for moleskins –
beneath his new class. *They ponged
of shirehorse. A pair'd fetch the dogs
to you for miles.* Dozens still hung
in Ludlow shops, framing the doors
with chains of pails and sieves,
rough wear for unluckier lads.

In his version of pastoral,
women kept up an image of order,
having their sprained ankles quietly away
in the city. Faces watched from nets,
greening behind geraniums. *None
of that now,* we say, meeting again,
*no more house-arrest;* then laugh
to think we've caged ourselves
in brick, claws kept trimmed, singing
for a salary, cuckooing on the hour –

until an old voice hisses in the head:
*Here you are, this generation,
luckiest of women since the Fall*
(according to the keeper of the gates)
*– and still reaching for more?*

Dredging old tales up from his past,
we feel the loss of what has been
suppressed – animal energy, perhaps,
but with it fear and danger. Back then,
down unmapped lanes on the green
and pagan edge of Herefordshire
where bully wars bled sap and gangs
stripped off each other's bark, I learnt
to spit out words like blow-darts. And you,
a cousin fresh from the city, politer in voice,
so perfectly sensible and not amused by
my best tall tales, I led into a field of cows
(bullocks, perhaps) and left. As you recall,
though I have only a bad memory of you
reminding me about it. At least you weren't
the girl I pushed off the bridge, an enemy,
not family like you, one of the tribe. But
we were set up as models for each other;
feuds came out of it: after a GCE draw,
degrees and so forth, teaching together.

We wrote ourselves out of the old script,
morality play with interludes of farce.
Hearing more sophisticated fables,
we shut our early book of beasts;
but we're still unseasoned, green at the core.
Secretly reading Arden editions of Eden,
we try out supposes of milkmaid selves
on pasteurized farms.

His tales were fact and fiction,
his telling was different truth,
which I'm putting down here for you
to cancel the cows,
now that my mother no longer
swears me to decency and silence,
and your father has no more words.

# Robe Shop

Two wigs on sticks,
both legal. A performs
tight loops on horseback
in close questioning; B's
florid and rhetorical, rolling
hair cigars to fire the brain.
This month 10% off
wig-tins, blue-bags.

Old mahogany shades
three bottles of fern cologne,
distilling cool green tropics
by a panama hat. Words
on the cards are obsolete:
*bespoke* and *gentleman's.*

Club ties fan out
round the block and gavel;
make yourself heard. Behind glass
there's a sliding morgue of linen.
Shirts lie stiff in trays, beheaded.
Sharp new moons of collar.
Against all this sobriety,
a robe stands apart:

*Oxford Doctor of Music,*
*Ivory-flowered Silk Damask*
*with Bright Cerise Pink Facings,*
the shocking pink of carnival.

Rank and degree, freemasonry
of knowledge. Women passed by
for years, but robes are now
hired out to *M* or *F* impartially.
Sawbones and justices, we're
through the window, hooded,
sworn in, though putting on
the old male style of Bachelor
or Master. Curious,

yet think of all that earlier
cross-dressing – fine brocades
and cherry linings, once in fashion,
later kept as robes for wedding
men to manly disciplines, though
wisdom, like the muse, was *f*
not *m* in gender. Outside, even
now, clerks run to their courts
and chambers, letters knotted
in pink ribbon called red tape.

# Balloon

A white loaf risen
over the suburb
sets the dogs off –
striped brioche,
bun with graffiti
swollen out of its
wicker basket –
BUILDING
a capital
SOCIETY.

Crick-necked,
reading the signs
from windows
or new gardens,
the mortgaged
watch its captives
feed the flame –
a gingerbread
oven's jammed
between chimneys.

It escapes
with a gas-hiss –
ogre breath –
fires off, and lifts,
PROPERTY
a shrinking
blue legend,
never-never
household tale.

Grounded,
stuck below
raw brickwork
(heavier now
the raising
AGENT's
lost its fizz),
closing doors
and windows,
crowds alone
spike bloated bills,
stare at ceilings,
juggle noughts,
or try old spells
for debts,
debtors,
daily bread.

# Post-War Almanac

As prophesied
after the long war –

years of shooting stars –
a change of weather.

To appease the new god
bronze images were melted,

days axed from the week.
A sign came:

oil rose through water,
blackening the shore.

Let out again, the sun
deposited its gold.

Brittle with drought,
the map split,

tilting houses off the earth.
Livestock at market

panicked, leapt fences;
the seed grew sour.

Swollen with air,
the hungry run to St Luck's.

Her gospel is written in light,
moving green oracles.

This day is her feast;
her chapel's stacked

with paper hearts,
the valentines of prayer.

Tinfoil, plaster,
she's drawn through the streets;

her banner's an eye
sewn up with gilt thread.

Suitors ride the floats
pricking gut balloons;

for those who fall
under the covered wheels

she does not intercede.

# The Feet

The new philosopher
at our clinic thought about
my spare feet,

bloody stumps from a dream.
The problem, I said, was storage.
They might be of use in future,

but veins kept shooting up
on the carpet, toes curled
in despair. Try a shrink,

he said. But they'd all gone
bobbing downriver when
the NHS floodgates burst.

Had I tried the lottery clinic,
Art for the Heart? They did a
course on Magritte. Tunnels

and trains. Don't give me that,
I said. Feet, not fetish. I'm being
dreamt, or it's that Jungian

thing. Everyone's waking up
to hear teeth rattling into
the sink. Kids watch granny

coming apart at the seams.
Our new philosophy, he said,
cures this mass delusion; it's

an abstract art, like politics.
Think of the extra feet as
Subject, not Object, being

unreal. I let them kick his shins,
but he wouldn't play: madwife
in need of community care.

Either you've sold out, I said,
or you're a fraud. Bet you can't
tell Hegel from Schlegel. Go on,

define epistemology.
He coughed; it's a job.
Did a retraining scheme

when insurance crashed, on
Time and Free Will at Work.
So, was I myself again?

That night I crept out;
dumped the feet on a tip,
left them by a packing-case,

like old boots, airing.
The box began to shake.
It said FROST-FREE

SIX CUBIC FEET CAPACITY.

# Annual

Never drawn to life, he watched her
training a rose. High on nitrates,

thin sticks cracked into leaf,
neon came to a head and burst.

His mind was shrubbery; sober privet
spread where bleeding hearts had once

dripped under the Gloire de Dijon. Alone
she fought the leaf-rolling sawfly, cutter-bee,

rust pustule, worm in the bud, while he
read on a striped chair facing the house.

Territorial border-patrols
make suburbs bloom in unison –

double cherry, laburnum. Roses tell
their brilliant perennial lie,

but growths resistant to pruning
sucker in flesh, sap it away.

Her scattered ashes made earth breed
again; bastard stock of sweet-briar

rambled about. Over the fence he saw
oiled bodies on airbeds, burnt to sienna,

cracking apples with their own teeth. House-
-bound, the carpet's tendrils writhed in corners.

Winter to come. He felt the gold band slide
knuckle to knuckle over slack skin, foresaw

uncoupling of bones. In the greenhouse,
clearing poisons out, he touched

a leather claw; her mould gripped
at damp. He poured sluggish dregs

into a jar, opened the deck-chair –
cobwebbing rotten, ratchets stuck –

sat in rain, and took his systemic,
cautious, drop by drop.

His double vision: grass greener
than any rose was red. An unfolding.

air got between packed layers, thin as gold leaf,
and blew them apart; he was yeasty.

Ropes coiled out of knots; dry ponds
turned to fountains, waterfalls;

stones caught fire and melted earth.
Appalled by such excess, he cut

the living daylights out. Flesh crept
down to its sunken garden.

# Monteverdi

Coils and loops of music
turn in their shell:
the long-forsaken *ninfa*
agrees with Philomel
that love is hell.

Courteous shepherds, vying
to offer ease,
echo her, *miserella*;
their modulating keys
don't please.

In sympathetic quavers,
fountains weep;
air records her grievance.
Chastened, she sinks to sleep,
numbering sheep.

Pastoral's a fiction;
urban decay
crawls over the meadow –
sister, come away.
Rewind, replay.

# Midsummer

Telling the shrub roses, *bold it*
*one more day  and you'll get*
*my full attention,* counting up

hundreds of loose pink
cabbages, hybrid musks, and
weak-necked purple Bourbons

smelling of cheap soap –
all of them bursting and blown
in the Junes lost to exams

taken or marked, marked,
since I was eleven – *Wait!*
I order the longest day,

but the year's going.
The apple miscarries
an early crop, honesty pods

take slides of darkening cells,
and the blackbird's too fagged
to sing after stuffing its young.

Everything blazes, goes,
and I haven't seen it,
reading these scripts about

high romantic vision,
eyes full of ink. Span
of attention's too short

(someone shaving a lawn,
the ice-van coming) to hold it.
Next life, be ready.